EMP(
TO ENʊᴀʊᴇ

MARRIAGE DONE RIGHT IS *HARD* WORK

(But It's Worth It!)

A 31-Day Guide to Put the Fun,
Fire and Focus Back in Your Marriage

Tony & Nicole Davis

CONTENTS

INTRODUCTION

In marriage, no topic should be off-limits. In fact, our inability to discuss the hard topics serves as a catalyst for communication breakdown, mistrust, and divisive behavior being displayed between spouses in today's society. Sometimes it's hard to talk, and we get that. We've been learning (and still are learning) how to best communicate, to be considerate, and to love one another in a way that exemplifies the teachings of the Bible.

As you read this devotional together, take your time, remove all distractions, and be prepared to hear one another from a deeper place. As you go through these pages, let each day bring you closer together as you learn more and more about the one you love. The knowledge inside is ageless, and you'llget something new and impactful every time you read it. This book is based on biblical principles; yet anyone, regardless of their faith, can use it to gain greater insight into a better marriage.

This easy-to-read book is designed to be interactive. For each day, you are provided a guiding scripture (New King James Version unless otherwise noted), a practical life application summary with additional scriptural references, and discussion questions or considerations. While this book is organized as a 31-day devotional, it can easily be utilized as a31-week devotional. The key is to make sure that you and your spouse completely address each topic and the questions presented before moving on to the next one. Some of the themes are repetitive by design. These are hallmark marriagetopics that serve as the glue and foundation to strong, healthy relationships. Lined pages are provided for note-taking after each day, to allow you to capture your action items, thoughts and ideas. Before you begin your daily marriage review, purpose yourself to fully participate. We encourage you to willfully

1

embark upon this journey and allow the healing power of God's Word to strengthen your marriage a little or a lot. We truly hope you are challenged and encouraged. Longlive strong marriages!

1

LET'S HAVE SOME FUN

The thief comes only in order to steal and kill and destroy.
I came that they may have and enjoy life, and have it in
abundance [to the full, till it overflows].

John 10:10 (AMP)

The lyrics of a song by Kool and the Gang say, "Let's burn up the night baby. Let's do it *together.* Let's have big fun." And, then the chorus says "Have some fun!" Jesus said that He came so that we may have and enjoy life. Does having and enjoying life equate to an existence that is devoid of fun?

You and your spouse are one. Vows were made to be together until death. As "mature adults," we make sure that we prioritize and give attention to the essential things such as our careers, children and finances. Doing so usually consumes most of our days and weeks and years. And, as Christians, we certainly know how to prioritize our ministries, whether full-time or as volunteers. But, have we considered the fact that Jesus said that He came so that we could **have and enjoy life**? On that note, shouldn't we prioritize our marriage too being intentional to spend time and have fun with our beloved spouse?

Let's also consider the verse in Ecclesiastes 3:12 (AMP) which reads, *I know that there is nothing better for them than to rejoice and to do good in one's lifetime.* Having fun will lead to a merry heart, and a merry heart does the body well like medicine (Proverbs 17:22).

3

Let's make having fun a priority. And, as the song also says, we are going to *do it together.*

Questions/Considerations:

1. As a Christian, you understand that you would go to heaven if you died tonight. That's certainly good news. Now, give some consideration to the abundant life you want to have with your spouse when you wake up tomorrow. Go ahead and plan some fun. It's OK.

_____

_____

_____

_____

2. Allow your planning to be fun. It should not be stressful. Choose a day, week, or month and organize an activity you are willing to lead. Perhaps there are events you'd like the two of you to attend. Coordinate the details for that activity/event on the note pages provided.

_____

_____

_____

_____

Notes

Notes

2

TRUTH AND LOVE ARE A LOVELY COUPLE

Instead, speaking the truth in love, we
will grow to become in every aspect the
mature bodyof him who is the head, that is,
Christ.

Ephesians 4:15 (NIV)

Do you find it difficult to be honest with your spouse? Difficult conversations about the direction, needs, decisions to be made, and challenges in a marriage can be intensified when you don't quite know how to phrase what's on your mind. Truth, coupled with love, can make things more palatable. Yes, both truth and love are needed.

You do yourself a disservice when you try to love in a situation where you cannot communicate any truth. The reality is that, in far too many cases, one or two scenarios usually play out. The spouse holds everything in and becomes very frustrated. Or, the truth does get communicated; however, it gets communicated to someone other than your spouse. As a result,you may get advice about how to *deal with him*, but you may not obtain the desired change you'd prefer to see.

Truth without love is extremely toxic. Brash delivery will result in a defensive recipient, who feels accused and attacked. And, when a person feels attacked, the reaction is to defend himself/herself instead of listening to the intention of the message. This is true even when the purpose of the delivery was not meant to be mean.

Considering the words in 1 Corinthians 13, love is patient and kind amongst other things. By taking time to consider your words in advance, practice them, then pray, you will stand a better chance of your spouse being able to hear your concerns with an open heart. Remember to check your motivation, your emotions, and your desired results; then ask God to help you choose the best words that will allow Him to be glorified, even in serious or hard conversations, as you couple truth and love in your communications.

Questions/Considerations:

1. What is the hardest part about being honest with your spouse?

_____

_____

_____

_____

2. How can you work together to overcome the barriers to managing difficult conversations?

_____

_____

_____

_____

Notes

Notes

3

YOU ARE NOT MY ENEMY

*Have I therefore become your enemy
because I tell you the truth?*

Galatians 4:16

"Oh, how I love thee. Let me count the ways." "I'll give my left arm for you. Heck, I love you soo much that I'll give my life for you!" "You are absolutely wonderful to me." "You mean the world to me." It's really easy to be starry-eyed and even extol your spouse when they sing your praises and lets you know how wonderful you are.

However, inevitably, somewhere, sometime, somehow, *life* outweighs the glorious clouds of wedded bliss. Then BAM! The bliss becomes blisters. You wonder what was so wonderful. And, you want your left arm back. It is in the difficult times that we are presented with an opportunity to discuss an imperfection—and we gladly take advantage of the opportunity.

"Honey, we'll need to alter our schedules if we are going to grow the business." "We will have to modify our spending and investing if we are going to have a good retirement or send the children to college." "You are not going to get six- pack abs if you keep eating junk food!" "Baby, your response was wrong in that situation and you may want to apologize.""Your relative has stayed with us long enough; it's time for them to find their own place."

Regardless of how simple or intense these truths are, most of the time we simply do not want to deal with their reality. But, the fact of the matter is that they have to be dealt with. The fact that your spouse communicated this truth to you is because it is consuming his/her mind space.

So, the real question is, how will you view your spouse for presenting you with this truth? Are you going to remember that he/she is the precious gift that God has allowed to unite with you? Or, are you going to discount God's gift and make your spouse *pay* for presenting you with an opportunity to address an issue? We already know how we should answer those questions. Now, let's demonstrate what we know.

Questions/Considerations:

1. When your spouse presents you with truth, do you think the intention is to help you? Or, do you think that your spouse is intentionally trying to harm you? Explain or write down your answers for discussion.

_____

_____

_____

_____

2. Are there steps or methods you can employ that will help you to receive truth from your spouse? If so, discuss or write down what they are.

_____

_____

_____

_____

Notes

Notes

4

THOUGHTS ARE SEEDS— WATCH WHAT YOU PLANT

*bringing every thought into
captivity to the obedience of
Christ...*

2 Corinthians 10:5

The old adage, "A family that prays together, stays together"is true. However, prayer alone is not enough. Because we are inundated with good and bad images all day, every day, we must support our prayers with making wise choices.

Our ability to control the images and the resulting thoughts that enter our minds will determine the kind of seeds that can take root. If you sow negative thoughts, with each corresponding negative thought, you water those seeds. If you sow good thoughts, with each corresponding good thought, you water those seeds.

It may sound easier said than done, but here is the challenge: be selective in what you choose to entertain as a thought. If the thought is not pleasing, uplifting, or glorifying God, arrestit, and dismiss it. Do it often and do it quickly. If you realize that your thoughts are often negative or destructive, seek help. You cannot heal what you do not first acknowledge.

We are spirit, soul, and body. Every aspect of our being must be nurtured and developed. The Bible is clear that there should be times of separation for fasting and prayer. The wise way to accomplish this is by designating a time of consecration along with your spouse. It is ideal to fast and pray together so that there is unity in what you are pursuing God for. Allow fasting and prayer to be a time to strengthen your marriage. Listen for what the Holy Spirit has to say during your time of consecration and then obey His instructions.

Questions/Considerations:

1. What accountability do you have in place with your spouse, your church, or your friends to help keep you from entertaining negative thoughts?

_____

_____

_____

_____

2. Is fasting a challenge? If so, what can you do to overcome this challenge?

_____

_____

_____

_____

Notes

Notes

5

YOU SHALL HAVE WHAT YOU SAY

Death and life are in the power of the tongue,
And those who love it will eat its fruit.

Proverbs 18:21

My God is omnipotent! Surely, he can breathe life into my marriage. After all, He's GOD!

Notwithstanding that fact, do you realize that God has granted YOU the power to impact your world? That power is right in your mouth. You can use your tongue to either create death or life. The choice is yours.

"I am wasting my time." "He'll never change." "I am just going to keep my mouth shut because she won't listen." The list is endless. These are negative and destructive words.

Conversely, you may say, "Baby I love you and I want the best us." "I want us to continue to grow and get better." These are positive and uplifting words. Self-fulfilling prophecy is dangerous and glorious. It happens in direct correlation with our beliefs and behaviors. When we speak our beliefs, and conduct ourselves in ways that support our ideas, we will experience the power of what we have said.

If you want growth, think about what you say and how to say it to create your world. If you think that your relationship lacks life, consider what you've said to create that lack.

You may want God to fix it. And, you may even be asking, "Where are you Lord, in my situation?" Truthfully, you may even be a little angry because God doesn't appear to be responding to your issue.

There are many proverbs that talk about the wisdom of appropriately using words. For this devotional, consider Proverbs19:3(NLT) which states that "people ruin their own lives by their own foolishness and then are angry with the Lord." (Proverbs19:3 AMP). Know that God has given you the power to create *your* world with *your* tongue.

If you've been foolish with your words, repent as quickly as possible. Ask for God's forgiveness. Ask for your spouse's forgiveness. Discuss and decide to make changes regarding how you talk to each other. And, talk about what constitutes proper communication between the two of you going forward.

Questions/Considerations:

1. In what ways do you need to change what you believe and say about your spouse and your marriage?

_____

_____

_____

_____

2. Take this time to pray together, asking God for healing and forgiveness over past words and deeds that may have hurt your spouse and your marriage.

_____

_____

_____

_____

Notes

Notes

6

SEX—GOD'S MASTER PLAN

Nevertheless, because of sexual immorality, let each man havehis own wife, and let each woman have her own husband. Let the husband render to his wife the affection due her, and likewise also the wife to her husband. The wife does not haveauthority over her own body, but the husband does. And, likewise the husband does not have authority over his own body, but the wife does.

1 Corinthians 7:2-4

Let's talk about sex! After all, the Bible sure does. Sex does not have to be a sticking point in a marriage, nor does it have to be used as a prize or a weapon. Marriage is most enjoyable when both spouses' needs are being met throughout the marriage and in daily activities. And, yes, those needs include sexual needs. "But, our libidos aren't in sync." That means you are a typical couple. Regardless, talk about it to obtain understanding, so you are aware of your spouse's wishes.

Women, please understand that desire for sex without foreplay or affection does not make your husband a depraved individual. Unromantic, yes. A weird man, NO. While your libido may not be as strong as his (in most cases), don't make him feel out of line for wanting you, though you may be thinking, "He *always* wants it!" It's not *always* because, every now and then, he gets into Rapid Eye Movement (REM) sleep and he may not be thinking about you. Know that he doesn't have a problem that needs to be fixed. You have the gift of sex, and that gift makes him desire you over, and over, and over, and over. Do you get the picture?

Men, understand that while your wives may be impressed with you, other things may take priority over seeing you and *wanting* you. When her security is threatened, her sexual desire goes down. And, non-sexual holding and affection will make her more receptive to sexual holding and affection.

We ask men and women to understand why we want or don't want sex. The understanding is in the facts. The reality is that most women will never comprehend the sex drive of a man. And, most men will never understand the affection needs of a woman. Regardless, it's beneficial to accept that those needs exist and that they are important, even if they donot make sense to you.

No one should treat sex as a drudgery, duty, or even a demand. Sex should be a loving exchange between husband and wife because you love one another and it is the ultimate expression of oneness. Sex is easily accomplished if there are no other competing demands such as careers, children, homework, sporting events, chores, and the like. Although these areas must be attended to, you can still show care for one another by setting a sex schedule that's practical and sustainable (with flexibility built in as needed). For your scheduled intimacy, make it fun, make it special, and make ita regular occurrence. This will ensure that both of your needsare being met.

Questions/Considerations:

1. What challenges do you have with being intimate with your spouse?

_____

_____

_____

_____

2. What do you need from your spouse to allow you to be fully engaged in your scheduled intimate times? This is a great time to take notes!

_____

_____

_____

_____

Notes

Notes

7

SUPPORT IS A TWO-WAY STREET

...submitting to one another in the fear of God.

Ephesians 5:21

Who's the boss? Him? Her? Is it a point of contention? Do you fight for control? Does requiring your spouse to submit give you the right to boss them around so you can have your way?"I'm the man and she needs to submit to me (yet you're also thinking, "Never mind the fact that she has way more knowledge than me in this area)." "I am a woman and we are supposed to submit to one another according to Ephesians 5:21 (even though you quote a scripture, you're thinking, "I'll never defer to him, despite the fact that I desire him to take the lead and to make decisions)."

Here's a thought. God is the boss and you're not—and we should all strive to do things *His* way.

Men, strive to be the quality of man that she would have no problem listening to. Let her know that you are a man who seeks the wisdom of the Word and who listens to the voice of the Holy Spirit in prayer. Then, let your actions be a demonstration of this confession.

Women, demonstrate your competence with humility. Men compete with other men. So, if you come off like a man, he'll compete with you too. Often, when dealing with men, how you say it is more important than what you actually say. Know that he wants a wife, not another

28

mother. So be mindful of your approach.

One of the most powerful aspects of marriage is that we have a live in cheerleader. We have someone always at our side who will help us conquer the cares of life, who will support us as we pursue our dreams and aspirations, and who will partner with us to address the most difficult conflicts and tragedies we may ever face. Support should be provided by both spouses.

In the Kingdom, the Bible tells us that God is no respecter of persons (Acts 10:34) and He doesn't show favoritism (Romans2:11). If you are modeling your marriage after Christ, then neither spouse should treat the other as if one person's job, interests, or obligations are more important than the other's. To ensure everyone's needs are being met, the wise thing to do is have a conversation to plan the best way to support one another. There are times when one person's wants or needs may need to be addressed more urgently than the others; but, as a rule of thumb, everyone's schedule and goals deserve attention.

Questions/Considerations:

1. What plan can be established to show support for the individual interests of both spouses?

_____

_____

_____

2. What are the barriers that keep both of you from fully supporting the other?

_____

_____

_____

Notes

Notes

8

YOU ARE HEIRS TOGETHER

Husbands, likewise dwell with them
with understanding, giving honor to the
wife, as to
the weaker vessel, and as being heirs together
of the grace of life, that your prayers may not
be hindered.

1 Peter 3:7

Being joint heirs makes you both royalty. What a concept! This means you are truly kings and queens in the Kingdom of God. What is your current perspective on your spouse? Do you see him as a king? Do you see her as a queen? Why or why not? These are very poignant questions to challenge your current mental and emotional position in your marriage.

Husbands, learning to know the personality of your wives will save you much heartache. There are two primary ways to do this. One way is to ask her directly. When seeking to understand your wife, inquire in a way that demonstrates that your ultimate desire is to please her. There are no guarantees that you'll completely comprehend her answers.

This is especially true when you process her response(s) through your male filter. Another way to get to know her is to observe her. Watch what she does, how she does it, and when she does it. Then, observe to discover why she does it.

The next best thing to do is to pray for your wife according to the Scriptures. Your wife has been placed at your side as a joint heir of the Kingdom of God. What the two of you can accomplish together is far more than what either of you can accomplish individually. You are stronger, smarter, and more effective as long as you work together, operating on one accord. Your perspective of your marriage will determine its success or failure. King, guard your thoughts, seek to understand, and give honor to your queen. It is not wise to voluntarily put yourself in a position where your prayers are hindered.

Questions/Considerations:

1. Wives, clearly explain what would make you feel more honored.

   _____

   _____

   _____

   _____

2. Husbands, if there is something you would like to know to help you understand your wives better, ask now. Use your notes to capture what you learn.

   _____

   _____

   _____

   _____

Notes

Notes

9

SUBMISSION IS NOT AN OPTION

Wives, submit to your own husbands, as is fitting in the Lord.

Colossians 3:18

As Christians, when we surrendered our lives to the Lord Jesus, we, in essence, gave up our rights to govern our own lives according to our own knowledge. What we agreed to dois read our Bible, obey God's commands, and follow the Holy Spirit's leading. As part of following God's commands, wives are to accept the leadership of their husbands. No other voicesupersedes the voice of your husband's as it relates to how your homes will be governed.

This can be a major challenge in a marriage for a number of reasons. Some of which include the way you were raised, thekind of relationship you had with your father (or lack thereof), or your unwillingness to live unselfishly and join your life fully to your husband's. It is the husband's responsibility to seek God's direction through prayer and Bible reading to ensure he is leading according to the will of God for the family. As wives, you cannot dictate what that looks like; you can only watch for the results.

Make no mistake, the responsibility of leading is not to be taken lightly. With leading comes accountability. Husbands will give an account to God for how well or how poorly the home is managed. This is the role men signed up for when they chose to get married. And wives, submitting to your husband's leadership and authority is what you signed up forwhen you said, "Yes."

Questions/Considerations:

1. What does submission "fitting in the Lord" look like in your marriage according to the Scriptures?

_____

_____

_____

_____

2. Discuss how to align your definitions of submission, as joint heirs, so that it works for the needs of your family.

_____

_____

_____

_____

Notes

Notes

10

IF YOU SAY IT, HONOR IT

*"I have made a covenant with my
eyes; Why then should I look upon a young
woman?"*

Job 31:1

Who you *really* are is the person you portray when no one else is
looking. Do you like that person? Is that person exemplifying Christ?
Is that person honoring covenants? Is that person honoring
commitments? If you cannot answer an emphatic YES to these
questions, you are able to see areas for growth and maturity especially
as it pertains to your behavior towards the opposite sex. No need to be
hard on yourself. Make a covenant to do better, then honor the
covenant. Here's how you can start this transformation. Repent. Then,
reject doing anything in private that you cannot or would not do or say
in front of your spouse.

Also, today is a great day to change your perspective on how you
handle the promises you've made or will make to your spouse and to
yourself. Once you make a covenant with your eyes and any other
aspect of your being, keep it. Be a man or woman of your word so that
deeper trust is built and expectations can be properly managed. Make a
covenant with your own eyes. It's important because, controlling your
eyes will control your heart (Matthew 5:27-28). Live a life where you
can encourage others to pattern their lives after yours (Philippians
3:17).

Questions/Considerations:

1. Is keeping your word challenging? If so, why?

   _____

   _____

   _____

   _____

2. How can your spouse assist you?

   _____

   _____

   _____

   _____

Notes

Notes

11

SEARCH FOR THE GOOD THINGS
IN YOUR SPOUSE

Finally, brethren, whatever things are true, whatever thingsare noble, whatever things are just, whatever things are pure,whatever things are lovely, whatever things are of a good report, if there be any virtue and if there is anything praiseworthy—meditate on these things.

Philippians 4:8

Some things qualify for thought. And, some things don't. Philippians 4:8 provides instruction on what qualifies for thought. Therefore, I will think thoughts such as, "My spouseis a blessing from the Lord. My spouse only desires to see me do well and is willing to help me through anything. My spouse seeks to do what's best for our family." These are all affirming, lovely, and praise-worthy thoughts to meditate on.

If you notice, what you think about and rehearse the most, is what you will experience in your life. If you say, "I'm looking forward to going home," you set your expectations towards positive reasons to be home such as, "I get to share quality time with my spouse;" "I can help out around the house;" "I can be around to influence the children;" "I can create some memories with my family."

Some may say, "My spouse is driving me crazy!" Well, were they crazy when you married them? Did you go into marriage thinking that you'd be in love for a little while and then get tired of each other by the seven-year itch? Absolutely not! You focused on their positive qualities despite their flaws. Today, they are still a flawed individual with some good qualities (just like you).

By staying focused on what's good, what's working, and what's important, you decrease the amount of negative energy available for toxic and debilitating thoughts against your spouse. In addition to changing thoughts, work on communicating your needs with your spouse. Oftentimes, our spouses are not aware they are doing things that cause us angst or dissatisfaction in the relationship.

Questions/Considerations:

1. List five things that you love about the way you and your spouse relate to one another.

2. List five things that you love about the way your spouse relates to others.

Notes

Notes

12

MARRIAGE HAS A DESTINATION

Where there is no vision, the people
perish:but he that keepeth the law,
happy is he.

Proverbs 29:18 (KJV)

If you're already married and have been for more than one year, it is a bit late to consider the pros and cons of marrying your spouse. However, if you are recently married or not married, pay close attention. Beyond sexual fulfillment, God has a plan for your marriage. Beyond having children and living in a "nice neighborhood," God has a plan for your marriage. In everything that God does, there is an element of*multiplication* (Genesis 1:28, Mark 10:30), *process* (Genesis 8:22), and *completion* (Jeremiah 29:11). Not only is there a plan for your marriage, but also your individual God-given assignment compliments what He wants to accomplish through you collectively.

The only way to discover God's plan for your marriage is to seek His face with regular prayer and fasting. He will also reveal and confirm His plan for you through your spiritual leaders and mentors. Knowing God's plan gives you greater ammunition against outside forces designed to destroy your relationship.

Also, when you realize the plan God has for your spouse, you will use your words more carefully and you'll treat your spouse with greater care. It's sobering to realize you have direct involvement in seeing your

48

spouse's individual assignment fulfilled as well. And, don't forget the last part of the above scripture that states that happiness is associated with having a vision and doing what God says.

Questions/Considerations:

1. What do you believe God wants to accomplish in you individually?

_____

_____

_____

_____

2. What do you believe God wants to accomplish in you as a couple?

_____

_____

_____

_____

Notes

Notes

13

THE GOOD AND THE FAVOR DON'T ALWAYS COME EASILY

He who finds a wife finds a good thing,
And obtains favor from the Lord.

Proverbs 18:22

Every woman is not automatically wife material. Therefore, if a woman becomes a wife, God says, she is a good thing. She is good because she becomes a "help meet" for her husband. God determined very early that it is not good for man to be alone (Genesis 2:18 KJV). Yet, God was with man when he said that. It wasn't good for man to be alone, so he gave him a good thing. Hmmm...

The reminder here is that a husband must care for his wife with full recognition and understanding that she is a good thing given to him from God to make him better to enhance his productivity in the divine purpose of his existence. And, she brings a certain kind of favor from the Lord. The favor may be more identifiable for the husband who purposes to value his wife; supporting her as she fulfills her individual destiny, speaking well of her, treating her with honor, and providing for the home.

Many couples are not able to experience this scripture as written because it is believed that the benefits of marriage are automatic. Unfortunately, they are not. There is a great deal of human effort required by both spouses to achieve fulfillment in the relationship.

Marital work is ongoing and should be met with a sense of wonder, not grudgingly. The fulfillment and contentment that can be experienced in your union will be determined by how you handle one another on a daily basis. Your job, your kids, and your friends should not get the best parts of you. Learn to save those parts of yourself for your spouse. Since you're already working on choosing the right words to speak over one another, rejoice in knowing that the favor of God makes it easier for you to work through every one of your challenges.

Questions/Considerations:

1. Wife, ask your husband how you can better serve him. List responses.

_____

_____

_____

_____

2. Husband, ask your wife how you can better serve her. List responses.

_____

_____

_____

_____

Notes

Notes

14

UNITY IS DAMAGE CONTROL AND SEED FOR PROSPERITY

Can two walk together, unless they are agreed?

Amos 3:3

Can two walk together, unless they agree? Not effectively. Unity is important for all of us (John 17:11, 22, 23) and it is especially true for marriages. Why is unity so important to a marriage? Jesus said, "If a house is divided against itself, that house cannot stand" (Mark 3:25, NIV). Those words are strong enough for us to realize that, without unity, our marriage will not and cannot survive. There is no such thing as living separate lives under the same roof. If that's what you're doing, it's not a marriage God's way. It's marriage *your* way.

As Christians, we have an obligation to live marriage out in the way God designed it to be. We cannot create our own version of marriage and expect God to bless it. We walk in deception to believe that lie. If you desire to see your marriage last longer than predicted, overcome hurdles with grace, and experience years of joy and laughter with your mate, you *must* walk in unity. Unity is not achieved by prayer alone. It takes hard and continuous work on behalf of both the husband and the wife.

The investment level in seeing the marriage thrive must be shared. Spending time together, communicating what's on your minds and in your hearts, studying the Bible together, going to marriage conferences and marriage retreats, spending time with other couples, and having couples to mentor your marriage are all tools to combat division in your home. The hard question you must ask yourself is, "How desperately do I want unity with my spouse, and what price am I willing to pay to have it?"

Questions/Considerations:

1. What are you doing to create and sustain unity in your home?

_____

_____

_____

_____

2. What are you doing that may create division in your home?

_____

_____

_____

_____

Notes

Notes

15

PURSUIT AND UNITY

Therefore shall a man leave his father and his mother,
andshall cleave unto his wife: and they shall be one flesh.

Genesis 2:24 (KJV)

Leave and cleave. It's a nice rhyme and we love to quote it. But, to practice it, now, that's an entirely different ball game. And, in this game, you will have to get your jersey dirty. What exactly does it mean to cleave? The Hebrew word is *dabaq*, which means to pursue with energy. Yes, it means exactly what it says—*pursue with energy*. It's not a cursory thing.

Notice that the instruction was to the man to *dabaq*. It was not for the woman. Men, please do not interpret this as a sign of weakness. Take courage in the fact that your pursuit displays desire for your wife. She will love this! And, she will more than likely respond positively to your pursuit. Pursuing her will force you to get into her world. Doing so will cause you to sacrifice. You can trust the fact that she'll notice that you've sacrificed to come into her world without you telling her what you are doing. This bears repeating—pursuing your wife DOES NOT make you weak. It makes you a man who follows the instructions of God. And, it'll also make you a man who has less marital challenges than those who do not cleave. Word to the wise.

Cleaving is the prerequisite to becoming one flesh. One flesh is called unity and unity is powerful! You can accomplish anything when you

60

are unified (Genesis 11:6). Your commitment to oneness must become a way of life. Marriages, like cars, need to be maintained. Without regular check-ups, hidden problems will begin to manifest and cause greater problems that are sometimes irreparable. Determine as a couple how you'd like to maintain your oneness.

Questions/Considerations:

1. Does your understanding of oneness align with God's? Discuss.

_____

_____

_____

_____

2. What changes do you each need to make to protect the oneness of your marriage?

_____

_____

_____

_____

Notes

Notes

16

SELF-CONTROL PAYS DIVIDENDS

...add to your faith virtue, to virtue
knowledge, to knowledge self-control...

2 Peter 1:5-6

Lets' get down to brass tacks. Self-control requires discipline. One who is self-disciplined will do the right things, right away, whether or not he or she feels like it. Often, we defer to our humanity and justify not doing the right thing. So, because of our humanity, we take advantage of the circumstance to perform a desired act, contrary to the instructions of the Scriptures and the Holy Spirit.

You say, "I'm just going to let him have a piece of my mind!" Why do we do this? After all, it's been scientifically proven that telling your spouse off does not get him to see things your way. You've probably conducted this experiment a time or two, and you have witnessed the conclusion. As the husband, you think, "My humanity tells me that I can just show her that I am really ticked. So, I'll deny her the satisfaction of receiving my affection. And then, I'll demonstrate my displeasure by giving her the cold shoulder or the silent treatment." Likewise, that too is an experience that has never resulted in someone else coming around and seeing the wisdom of your position.

We are in complete control of our own actions. Yet, we are deceived enough to believe we can justify our actions by saying, "My spouse made me do it." Others will simply blame the devil. As we can clearly see, these actions do not demonstrate self-control. We spend so much time catering to our human nature we forget (to our own detriment) that we should be governed by the spiritual principles God has given to us in the Bible. Take this in. We are spiritual beings having a human experience. As a result, we should live in the Spirit and walk in the Spirit (Galatians 5:25, Romans 8:4-5). Get this settled in your mind.

Questions/Considerations:

1. Are there times when you try to justify acting in the flesh, contrary to the word of God?

_____

_____

_____

_____

2. What will you do to change?

_____

_____

_____

_____

Notes

Notes

17

TO WAR OR NOT TO WAR—IT'S STILL WARFARE

So letting your sinful nature control your
mind leads to death. But letting the Spirit
control
> *your mind leads to life and peace.*

Romans 8:6 (NLT)

Have you ever said, "I don't like what he did," "I don't like how she did it," or "I don't like how she said it?" If you have, like many couples, your misapplied conflict resolution skills probably tell you to keep your mouth shut so you can *keep the peace.* You resort to this method over and over again and obtain the same negative results. You think, "We are not fussing, so I am keeping the peace." This is self-deception. Not addressing issues does not lead to peace. It actually leads to the worst kind of warfare: the warfare that takes place right between your ears. The enemy accuses your spouse of whatever actions that make you irritated. You entertain those accusations and agree with the accuser about your spouse. Then, you become frustrated because you *have not* or feel that you *cannot* address your spouse about the issue. And, the enemy will tell you that you not addressing your spouse is your spouse's fault.

Do NOT let the enemy win! Ask the Holy Spirit to help you control your mind. The Bible gives clear examples for us in 2 Corinthians 10:5

and Philippians 2:5-11. Take the time to study and pray these scriptures over one another. Then, work towards having real peace in your home, in your relationship and in your mind.

Questions/Considerations:

1. Are there unresolved issues that you need to address?

   _____

   _____

   _____

   _____

2. Can you think of a respectful way to address those issues with your spouse? Use your notes sections to write your ideas.

   _____

   _____

   _____

   _____

Notes

Notes

18

COMPLIMENT WHAT SHE DOES

A man has joy in giving an appropriate answer,
And how good and delightful is a word spoken at the right
moment—how good it is!

Proverbs 15:23 (AMP)

Because of our familiarity with one another, we are often challenged with continually complimenting our wives. We get into the routine of life and become task-oriented. Sadly, it's easy to ignore or minimize what our spoken word means to the person we have chosen to dedicate our lives to. If anyone deserves to be treated with the utmost regard and respect, it is our wives.

There is a song by James Ingram, *"Find One Hundred Ways,"* which provides invaluable tips on what to do *and* what to say to make your wife feel special. We are really without excuse. It's not that we don't know what to do. If that were the case, you would not be married right now. We work hard to show our bosses, our friends, our pastors, and other people how wonderful we are, yet we put very little effort into consistently showing our wives why we are a great choice to have as a lifelong mate. Paying the bills and being there for the children are only partial elements of the equation. You had to do or say *something* complimentary (at least once) to get her to marry you. If you've stopped or have gotten complacent, find some new ways to compliment what she does!

Questions/Considerations:

1. In what ways do you compliment your wife and how often do you compliment her?

_____

_____

_____

_____

2. If compliments are important, how does it make you feel to not receive them? Both spouses can share answers for this question.

_____

_____

_____

_____

Notes

Notes

19

ACTIONS WILL ALWAYS BE
LOUDER THAN WORDS

*Believe Me that I am in the Father and the Father in
Me; or, else believe Me for the sake of the [very] works
themselves. [If you cannot trust Me, at least let these
works that I do in My Father's name convince you.]*

John 14:11 (AMP)

You've said it once, twice, or many times. You may have said, "I am
going to pray with you more." "I am going to take you out next
weekend." "I am going to spend more time with you when I come home
from work." I won't buy anything else." "We are going to have more
sex." Yet, your spouse still does not seem to believe you. You may even
be annoyed because you have been making a good faith effort for one
whole week!

Although it may be quite challenging to do, try not to take it personally.
Most people, including your spouse, will evaluate you and wait to see
how long you will keep up this act. Along with your words, there also
must be a behavior change. Think about it, if it is a *true* heart change,
there will be no need to look for an immediate reaction from your
spouse because *you* know you are different. The *new you* is here to stay
no matter what.

Now, you may still think that your spouse should automatically believe
you have changed simply because you've *said* you will pray, stop, help,

fix, give, be nice, not criticize…you can fill in the blank. And as the spouse who is trying to do better, you believe that's a reasonable expectation. But, consider how long you've been inconsistent with your behavior. Objectively speaking, is the request for your spouse's immediate acceptance really a reasonable request? After all, do you readily accept all her declarations the moment she makes them? If you want to prove your change is for good, show proof by your actions (Acts 26:20). Even Jesus said that He should not be believed unless He carried out the Father's work (John 10:37). And, we know from Scripture that Jesus was a man of action. He lived out His Word consistently every day.

Questions/Considerations:

1. What makes it difficult to believe what your spouse says?

_____

_____

_____

_____

2. How does it make you feel when your spouse does not keep promises?

_____

_____

_____

_____

Notes

Notes

20

RIGHTEOUSNESS BRINGS PEACE

And this righteousness will bring peace.

Isaiah 32:17 (NLT)

When we think about our marriage relationship, the aspects of it that make it hard are notoriously related to what the other person does or will not do. The enemy is successful in making you focus on all that is wrong, why this marriage isn't working, and how much better life would be *without* this other person in it.

Take a moment to take your most aggravating thought about your spouse and examine it from another angle. Say to yourself, "From now on, when my spouse does X, in order toshow that I am responding in a righteous manner, I will do Y." Romans 12:18 says, "If it is possible, as much as depends on you, live peaceably with all men." Whoa. Think about that.As much as depends on you is where your focus should be. Now, instead of focusing on the X, you need to focus on *your*

Y. The Y actually has a much bigger meaning because now we can look at the relationship. *Why* did you marry your spouse? *Why* is your spouse important to you? *Why* are you not doing everything, as much as depends on you, to live peaceably? If you're unable to have this level of peace, you may need to examine your level of righteousness and start thereal work right there in you.

Questions/Considerations:

1. As you reflect on your relationship with God and study these verses, how are you measuring up with living peaceably with your spouse? Use your book to write your response.

_____

_____

_____

_____

2. What are your *whys* for doing the best you can to work towards a stronger relationship with your spouse? Write your response.

_____

_____

_____

_____

Notes

Notes

21

SET THE TONE

Like apples of gold in settings of
silverIs a word spoken at the
right time.

Proverbs 25:11 (AMP)

We've all been there. We have an issue. The issue is with our spouse. The issue could be either major or immaterial. Regardless, today is the day, and now is the time that you will address this situation. Picture this scene: you are going to present the truth of the matter to your spouse. You are confident your spouse will receive it. After all, your spouse should want to know the truth so she can grow in the things of God. You know the truth will make your spouse free. As a result, you believe your spouse is going to have an obedient ear to what you are saying, so you know your rebuke will be welcomed according to Proverbs 25:12.

Now the scene changes. And what you envisioned is NOT the outcome you are confronted with. The conversation does not go as expected. In fact, it goes in a totally different direction and it all falls apart. Your take away may be that you regret even broaching the subject. You may even tell yourself that you'll never bring *that* up again!

But then, the truth hits you. You'll have to address it again. But, how? Remember, Proverbs 25:11 tells us that words can be spoken at the *right time*. So now, how do we discover that subjective *right time*?

Well, let's learn from God. We are clearly instructed on how to appropriately approach God. He wants us to come to Him with thanksgiving and praise (Psalm 100:4). Does that mean that we don't have frustrations or complaints? Of course not. But, what this does show us is that our approach will set the tone for the rest of the interaction.

Likewise, the way you approach your spouse will set the tone for the conversation. If you approach her with words of affirmation and praise, she will be receptive, and you'll enjoy your time with her. However, the converse is likewise true. If you approach him with accusations and complaining, receipt of your words will be hindered. So, keep this in mind as you approach your spouse. It is critical to start the interaction in a way that will make your spouse open to hear and receive what you have to say. If you take care to follow this prescription, you will appreciate the after effects.

Questions/Considerations:

1. Would your spouse say that you approach them with compliments and affirmations?

_____

_____

_____

_____

2. Discuss ways to appropriately approach your spouse.

_____

_____

_____

_____

Notes

Notes

22

YOUR SOUL NEEDS ATTENTION

keep working out your deliverance with fear and trembling

Philippians 2:12 (CJB)

Have you ever heard of the term *soul wounds*? Soul wounds are lesions, bruises, cuts, breaks, or burns that have occurred on the inside of us. These kinds of problems are not normally addressed in pre-marital counseling. Many times, it's hard to know that you carry them because you don't quite know howto identify them. Since you've had them most of your life, they seem to just be "who you are" or your personality make-up. Here is where the real challenge is presented to you.

This sort of self-assessment has nothing to do with your spouse; however, if you don't take the time to address your inner soul-related hurts, they will not only negatively impact you, they will also hurt your spouse, your children, and your friends. They could potentially destroy your career and your family overall.

Choice is powerful because you can use it to change. You can use it to stop. You can use it to get help.

The Bible is your number one place to receive inner healing. There are Scriptures to pray and to speak over your life so you can begin the process of moving in the right direction. There are times, though, where we may need to take our inner healing a step further and seek professional help. When you've tried all that you believe you can do but the pieces are still not coming together, your spouse can be your greatest advocate in walking with you through your darkest, toughest times to get the inner healing the Bible says we need to *work* for.

You *can* be healed. Getting healed by getting help gives you and your family better odds of making it through your storms to get to the other side. Getting help is your responsibility and your spouse can support you in the battle. We pray for the prosperity of your soul (3 John 1:2).\

Questions/Considerations:

1. Do you have behaviors that are causing your spouse and your family constant pain? If so, write them down for your review.

_____

_____

_____

_____

2. If you knew the right person to call, would you contact him/her to get help? Discuss possible options for who you could contact to receive the guidance and assistance you need.

_____

_____

_____

_____

Notes

Notes

23

APPRECIATION GRANTS
UNLIMITED ACCESS

Let your fountain be blessed, and rejoice with the wife of your youth. As a loving deer and graceful doe, let her breasts satisfyyou at all times; and always be enraptured with her love.

Proverbs 5:18-19

It's true, the longer we are married to our spouses, the easier it becomes to take each other for granted. You may notice you spend less time together, you're not checking on each other throughout the day (with a call or a text), you no longer play and laugh together, and you don't dream and make plans with one another in mind.

Appreciation for the little things will go a long way. A door opened, a kind word spoken, a meal prepared, a car washed, are all acts of love that warrant appreciation. You can also show appreciation by continuing to serve one another in ways that make you feel special and valued. *By doing these small things often, you create an environment of love and affection.*

By God's design, women are created to multiply what they've been given. A house becomes a home beautifully decorated; and, random ingredients (from the refrigerator, kitchen cabinets and anywhere else) can easily become a meal that looks like the one on page 78 of your favorite magazine.

When a husband shows appreciation to his wife for the way she cares for the home and for the family through his words, assistance, and random acts of kindness, he replenishes her energy and boosts her eagerness and readiness (if you understand the meaning here) to show him appreciation in the way he desires the most.

Please note, however, that appreciation goes both ways. When wives see their husbands supporting and partnering in this way, it is wise to celebrate and praise them for being present and connected. Be mindful not to take one another for granted.

Questions/Considerations:

1. What do you need from one another to create more time for sexual intimacy?

_____

_____

_____

_____

2. What are the two most time-consuming and energy-draining responsibilities you have? If appropriate, how can your spouse help?

_____

_____

_____

_____

Notes

Notes

24

HOW TO DETERMINE WORTH

*Who can find a virtuous
wife? For her worth is far
above rubies.*

Proverbs 31:10

Wives, exhale. There is no biblical requirement for you to become the exhaustive list as described in Proverbs 31. In order to accomplish this list, you would need a kingdom of your own, along with handmaidens, servants, and handlers. Until you're provided the requisite essentials to allow you to accomplish this list (as written), you can simply look to God to determine your worth.

Husbands and wives have been made in the image and likeness of God. He has given us access to everything we will ever need to please Him, to satisfy our spouse, and to fulfill God's calling for our lives.

Wives feel pressure coming from their husbands, friends, family members, the media, and even self-inflicted pressure to look, act, and perform in certain ways. This is enough to send women spiraling into depression and self-minimization that actually hinders her ability to hear from God.

Husbands, the best way to assist your wives is to remind them that they are *enough* and that you love them unconditionally. The Word of God properly applied will handle the rest.

Questions/Considerations:

1. Take this time to share any feelings or thoughts that can help you understand one another better.

   _____

   _____

   _____

   _____

2. How can your spouse support your efforts to overcome any issues you've discussed so far in this devotional?

   _____

   _____

   _____

   _____

Notes

Notes

25

THE ONLY PERSON WHO CAN HURT YOUR MARRIAGE IS YOU

So then, they are no longer two but one flesh.
Therefore, what God has joined together, let not a
man separate.

Matthew 19:6

When it comes to the stability of your marriage union, no person has the power to separate the two of you. That's right! We always hear talk of the "other man" or the "other woman," but they only get access to the relationship if you are willingly giving it to them. You must protect the family unit at all cost. Let no one separate you. And, *you* are included in that no one. Monitor your own behavior and pay attention to the warning signs. If you find yourself sharing intimate information about your spouse with someone from the opposite sex, or if you are engaged in behavior that would embarrass your family, you have the ability to choose to stop before things go too far. Nothing just happens.

So, if your thoughts, time, interests, and desires are no longer for your spouse, seek help. Do not be afraid to tell your spouse about your dissatisfaction in the marriage. Your spouse would rather hear, "I think we need help" than "I'm having an affair."

The best way to plan for the rocky times in your marriage is to talk about them while everything is going well in the relationship. Be receptive and active in establishing divorce- prevention steps. This will help you stay devoted to the marriage vows and the family unit even when times get difficult.

Questions/Considerations:

1. What aspects of the marriage, if any, are causing you to feel disconnected?

_____

_____

_____

_____

2. What do you need from your spouse to strengthen your connection?

_____

_____

_____

_____

Notes

Notes

26

WHAT'S IT LIKE TO BE MARRIED TO ME?

And just as you want men to do to
you, you also do to them likewise.

Luke 6:31

It's a very simple question. Would I want to marry someone who possessed my thoughts, actions, attitude, and tone? Do the introspection and make the necessary changes. There's no need to get down on yourself for not being perfect. Rather, bethankful that you've examined yourself and that you know exactly what you need to do to improve. Yes, the Scriptures instruct us to examine ourselves (2 Corinthians 13:5).

Marriage is a selfless commitment to another human being fort the rest of your life or theirs. Through marriage, you are able to learn ways of serving one another at the highest level, with Jesus as your example. If you endeavor to study the attributes of Jesus and apply them to your married life, you have the best opportunity to glorify God. When serving your spouse becomes difficult, the change that needs to occur lies within you.

Marriage done right is hard work, but it's worth it! It *can be* enjoyable. It is wise to relinquish all pre-conceived ideas about what your marriage should look like and be intentional about not falling into the trap of comparing your marriage to any other ones. People are different and the dynamics are different. There are risks in EVERY relationship.

Use the Word of God as your manual to establish what will make *your* marriage work best that is agreeable to both of you. By doing so, you will show your children, your family, and all others who are observing, what love and marriage looks like when it's done God's way.

Questions/Considerations:

1. Why does it feel like marriage is hard work?

_____

_____

_____

_____

2. Ask your spouse what they love most about your marriage so you can do those things more.

_____

_____

_____

_____

Notes

Notes

27

FREELY GIVE YOUR SPOUSE WHAT IS NEEDED

Nevertheless let each one of you in particular so love his own wife as himself, and let the wifesee that she respects her husband.

Ephesians 5:33

When you wake up in the morning, what are your initial thoughts about? Yourself? The children? Something else? When you prepare your daily, weekly, or monthly schedule, where does your spouse fit in with all that you need to accomplish?

The challenge is to put your spouse at the top of your list. After your time alone with God, your spouse should be next on your list not your children, not your friends, and not extra-curricular events that you have committed yourself to. By prioritizing your spouse, husbands show value and importance to their wives; and, wives show consideration and honor to their husbands.

Why is this so important? God has made us with emotional needs. Beyond the spiritual aspect of our lives, there is a very real natural component, the soul (our mind, will, and emotions) that should not be ignored. Both are extremely important to maintaining a strong marriage. Avoid the rut ofmaking your spouse earn your affection, or withholding your affection until your spouse shows affection first.

Daily, commit to paying close attention to your body language, your tone of voice, your level of patience, your availability to help out with family obligations, and your willingness to make sacrifices for one another.

Questions/Considerations:

1. Discuss your list of priorities and ask your spouse if he/she is getting what he/she needs from you.

_____

_____

_____

_____

2. Discuss what love and respect mean in your marriage.

_____

_____

_____

_____

Notes

Notes

28

PRAY FOR YOUR SPOUSE

*"You have heard that it was said, 'You shall love your
neighbor and hate your enemy.' But I say to you, love
your enemies, bless those who curse you, do good to those
who hate you, and pray for those who spitefully use you
and persecuteyou, that you may be sons of your Father in
heaven; for He makes His sun rise on the evil and on the
good, and sends rainon the just and on the unjust. For if
you love those who love you, what reward have you?"*

Matthew 5:43-46

If we are going to be honest, it is really hard to bless and pray for
someone that you do not like, not to mention doing righteous acts
toward your enemies! Nevertheless, God requires that we do just that.
He doesn't consider what they've done or how it impacted our lives.
The standard of God remains. Let's bring this home.

Oftentimes we "love" our spouses but we do not "like" them. And, when
we do not like them, we treat them as if they are our enemies, right?
It is a travesty to watch divorce proceedings. Here are two people
who vowed to love one another forever and yet, they are doing
everything within their power to cause the other as much pain and
damage as is legally allowed.

Do you ever wonder why God requires such a hard thing of us: to pray and bless our enemies? Could it be that He wants to protect our hearts? The Bible says out of our hearts flow theissues of life (Proverbs 4:23); and out of the abundance of theheart, the mouth speaks (Luke 6:45).

So, consider this, if you are constantly praying for your spouse no matter how you feel, no matter how you have been hurt, no matter what promises have been broken you can guard your heart against the toxic growth of hatred,bitterness, unforgiveness, cynicism, and ill-will towards them.

Also, the Bible teaches us that blessings and curses should not come out of the same mouth (James 3:10). This is serious to think about. To decide to pray heart-felt and scripturally- sound prayers for your spouse, no matter what, keeps your heart soft and open towards them even when you don't like what they've done or said.

Here is the other part to this matter. God will *always* love both of you. He shows no partiality towards one over the other (Acts 10:34). He sent Jesus to die for both of you. While you were both messy and living sinful lives, He chose you, to love you forever, and He *never* stops praying for you. Practice prayer. Practice prayer. Practice prayer.

Questions/Considerations:

1. While you are getting along, ask your spouse what type of things he/she would like prayer for. Commit to one another to pray for these topics every day no matter whator until the prayer is answered.

---

2. If you have not been praying for your spouse, make a fresh commitment to God and to your spouse to pray for them.

_____

_____

_____

_____

Notes

Notes

29

FORGIVENESS IS POWER AGAINST THE ENEMY

Now whom you forgive anything, I also forgive. For if indeed I have forgiven anything, I have forgiven that one for your sakes in the presence of Christ, lest Satan take advantage of us; for we are not ignorant of his devices.

2 Corinthians 2:10-11

What's the benefit of holding a grudge? Conduct your own research on the consequences of unforgiveness and medical effects on the body. Forgiveness is a weapon against the enemy of your marriage. Satan desires to see you, your spouse, and your children divided and ultimately destroyed. He hates love. He hates marriage and he hates unity.

When couples know the enemy's strategies and devices, and realize that he is always at work to destroy what God has ordained, which is the sanctity of marriage, they will better understand that the best thing to do for the longevity and strength of their marriage is to forgive one another quickly and often.

Jesus teaches us that we should not hold a grudge (Ephesians 4:31-32) and that we should forgive often (Matthew 6:14-15). The Bible says we will be forgiven *if* we forgive (Luke 6:37).

What keeps us from readily doing so is our pride and our emotions.

117

God does not consider our emotions when He tells us to forgive. He only considers the power we exude by trusting His biblical principles that are in place to keep us andour families safe from the evil one. Now, please understand, forgiveness does not mean you are condoning the behavior. Consequences will still follow every action or offense. But, extending forgiveness can free you from any additional trauma and pain.

Questions/Considerations:

1. What makes forgiving your spouse difficult to do?

_____

_____

_____

_____

2. What Bible verses about forgiveness can you meditate on to help you practice forgiveness?

_____

_____

_____

_____

Notes

Notes

30

TIME AWAY TOGETHER
REKINDLES THE RELATIONSHIP

"Draw me away with you and let us run together!"

Song of Solomon 1:4 (AMP)

Marriage Get-Away! It is absolutely necessary! This is not a family vacation. No children allowed! Create and protect these times away so the marriage can be rekindled. Time away doesn't always have to be a romantic setting. Be adventurous! The quoted scripture from Song of Solomon denotes running, which means, exerting energy through physical exercise! Certainly, you have not forgotten how to have fun with your spouse; it just needs to be planned. The very process of planning the trip can make you excited about going away together. It's even better when it's planned as a couple.

Here's something else for you to consider, these get-aways do not have to be expensive, nor do they need to be for long stints of time. It can be just as fun to steal away for a half-day! The length of time is negotiable. Consistency is key and variety adds spice.

Believe it or not, God created fun! Don't deprive yourselves of this precious element of marriage. It is understood how the cares of life can cause us to stop enjoying the sunshine and the flowers; however, our spouses can help us to remember how special time together can be. There's no better time than the present to start thinking about where you can go and what you can do.

Questions/Considerations:

1. What are ways to have fun (outside of the bedroom) that don't cost money?

_____

_____

_____

_____

2. What steps need to be taken in order to plan time away over the next 30 days?

_____

_____

_____

_____

Notes

Notes

31

STAY TEACHABLE

One who turns away his ear from hearing the law,
Even his prayer is an abomination.

Proverbs 28:9

No one likes being around a know-it-all. And, it's quite amazing how difficult it is for couples to ask for help. Just as amazing is how rigid spouses can be about changing bad behaviors, toxic thinking, and false beliefs regarding the Scriptures. The Bible admonishes us, in all our getting, to get understanding and seek wisdom (Proverbs 4:5-7).

We must remember that the greatest expression of our love for one another is our willingness to change *any* aspect of ourselves that hurts our spouses. It's a selfless act that is hardto accomplish. We wear our personalities as a badge of honor by making statements such as, "Well, this is just who I am." This kind of thinking serves to defeat our relationships. God requires us to be willing and teachable vessels—not just in our service to Him, but also in our service to one another. When there are disagreements about our roles in the relationship, how to handle a difficult situation, or the best way to parent the children, both spouses must agree to do what is best for the sake of all involved.

Arguments and disagreements based on *who* is right, will suffocate the marriage. Conversations based on *what* is right will protect the marriage.

Determine in your heart that you will work on being

open, and willing to grow, learn, and change. By doing so, you willplease the Lord and your prayers will not be hindered.

Questions/Considerations:

1. What about yourself would you like to change?

_____

_____

_____

_____

2. What can you do to begin to grow together as a couple?

_____

_____

_____

_____

Notes

Notes

More from Tony and Nicole Davis

Visit *www.empowertoengage.com* to learn more about Tony and Nicole, their ministry and other available resources. This *Done Right* devotional book series includes:

Parenting Done Right Is Hard Work (But It's Worth It!)

This 31- day guide helps parents navigate the challenging, stressful, yet rewarding role of parenting. It serves as a go-to handbook to help address some of the toughest issues we facein our increasingly not so child-friendly world.

Leadership Done Right Is Hard Work (But It's Worth It!)

This 31-day guide challenges every person to lead *themselves* first and provides the strategies to do so. How we make decisions, conduct ourselves, and interact with others are the ultimate tests to our level of success in every area of life. Improving yourself, will make you the person that others willwant to follow.

To invite Tony and Nicole to speak at your next event, contact them with details:

Phone: 1-800-345-0805

Email: info@empowertoengage.com

Website: www.empowertoengage.com

Facebook: www.facebook.com/empowertoengage/